A Programme for Schizophrenia

A PROGRAMME FOR SCHIZOPHRENIA

Jacqui Lee Schiff, M.S.S.W.
Joseph B. Kadane, Ph.d.
Charles Frohman, Ph.d.
Mark Schervish, Ph.d.
Judith Erb, M.S., Ph.d. candidate
David Kline, M.D.
Shea Schiff, M.A.
Laura Taub, M.S.W.
Ken Warner, B.S.

Published in 1990 by
The Self Publishing Association Ltd
Lloyds Bank Chambers,
Upton-upon-Severn, Worcs

in conjunction with
Cathexis Institute
P.O. Box 237,
Alamo, California.
USA.

British Library Cataloguing in Publication Data
A Programme for Schizophrenia
1. Man. schizophrenia
I. Schiff, Jacqui Lee
616.8982

ISBN 1 85421 073 4

Cover designed by Chris Redman.

Designed and Produced by The Self Publishing Association Ltd.
Printed and Bound in Great Britain by Billing & Sons Ltd, Worcester

Authors of Biochemical Paper

Jacqui Lee Schiff, M.S.S.W.

Founder of Cathexis Institute and Director there for eight years. Was also a founder of Transactional Analysis, the Athma Shakti Vidalaya in India, and Cathexis Europe, in the U.K. Author of several books and articles, and has received many honors. Still associated to Cathexis Institute and Cathexis Europe Ltd.

J. Kadane, Ph.d.

Chairman of Statistics Dept., Carnegie Mellon University, Pittsburg, Penn. for nine years. Presently holds a chaired professorship with that institution. Specializes in Bayesian statistics. Has written extensively and received many honours.

Charles Frohman, Ph.d.

Presently retired. Former Chairman of Biochemistry Dept. at Lafayette Clinic. Many publications. Specialized in biochemical psychiatry and seeking a biochemical defect associated to schizophrenia.

Judy Erb, M.S., Ph.d. candidate.

Biochemist, specialized in biochemical psychiatry. Previously employed at Lafayette Clinic.

David Kline, M.D.

Child Psychiatrist, trained at Stanford University. Co-director at Cathexis Institute for five years and Director for two years. Presently employed in the children's program at Napa State Hospital, Napa, California.

Mark Schervish, Ph.d.

Presently a professor of Statistics at Carnegie (described above) and is Associate Chairman of his department.

Shea Schiff, M.A.

Psychologist. Co-director of Cathexis Institute for five years. Specialized in treatment of schizophrenia and character disordered problems. Former renowned teacher of Transactional Analysis. Author and theoretician. Presently employed in business.

Laura Taub, M.S.W.

Social Worker and volunteer at Cathexis Institute.

Ken Warner, B.S.

Biochemist, employed at Lafayette Clinic. Specializes in biochemical psychiatry.

Contents

Let not young souls be smothered out before
They do quaint deeds and fully flaunt their pride.
It is the world's one crime its babes grow dull,
Its poor are ox-like, limp and leaden-eyed.

Not that they starve, but starve so dreamlessly;
Not that they sow, but that they seldom reap;
Not that they serve, but have no gods to serve;
Not that they die, but that they die like sheep.

Vachel Lindsay

Abstract

Evaluation of the progress of unmedicated schizophrenic patients at the Cathexis Institute (CI) in Oakland, California, indicated improvement toward normality as measured by the MMPI Scale 8, the level of tryptophan uptake in the blood, and an index of social functioning. With respect to tryptophan uptake, 55 patients were compared to 16 unmedicated schizophrenic patients in a research ward at the Lafayette Clinic (LC), Detroit, Michigan, and 15 nonschizophrenic staff at that clinic. A yearly cycle of tryptophan uptake peaking in late fall or early winter was discovered in all three samples. Neither the patients nor staff subjects at LC showed much trend over time in tryptophan uptake, but the LC patients' tryptophan uptake was higher than the LC staff. CI patients' tryptophan uptake dropped at such a rate that a CI patient's tryptophan uptake, hypothetically equal to that of the median LC patient subject, would drop to the level of the median LC staff subject in 32.7 months (5.4 months standard deviation) if such an extrapolation of the data were valid. Less dramatic but definite improvements were also present in the MMPI Scale 8 and in the Social Functioning Index.

Introduction

The relationship between the biochemical and the psychosocial life of the seriously mentally ill person is not yet well understood. There is evidence that biomedical treatments affect psychosocial outcomes. (Smith, Glass and Miller, 1980.) However, the question of whether psychosocial treatments can lead to bicohemical outcomes is largely unaddressed. The research reported here measures a biochemical outcome of a psychosocial treatment for schizophrenia. It evaluates a treatment program developed at the Cathexis Institute (Schiff, 1975) using tryptophan uptake (Frohman, Warner, Yoon, Arthur and Gottlieb, 1969) as a dependent measure.

Method

Overview

Fifty-five unmedicated patients in Cathexis Institute (CI), Oakland, California, were evaluated in three different ways: (a) by a standard psychological test (MMPI Scale 8 with K): (b) by clinical evaluation of social functioning, and (c) by a biochemical indicator (measurement of the influence of patients' blood on trypotphan uptake into chicken erythrocytes). The heterogeneity of schizophrenic populations cause experts to disagree concerning the reliability of any one of these indicators. Since it is unlikely that all three indicators would simultaneously show artifactual improvement, taken together they constitute a reasonable basis for evaluation.

With respect to tryptophan uptake these patients were compared to 16 unmedicated and no longer treated schizophrenic patients in a research ward at the Lafayette Clinic (LC), Detroit, Michigan, and 15 staff at that clinic. This poses a difficulty, since the assignment to treatment programs was not controlled. Initial differences among the patient groups are therefore potentially confounded with treatment effects.

The Minnesota Multiphasic Personality Inventory was utilized as the index of psychological functioning. This test was chosen because it was already familiar to the staff at both the Cathexis Institute and the Lafayette Clinic, and was judged by both groups to be suitable to this task. Since Scale 8 with K avoids interpreter bias, it was used in this study without profile interpretations. We refer to it below simply as Scale 8. No similar standard scale for social functioning was located that was appropriate for the CI population, since those available did not include a range of items descriptive of individuals whose functioning became normal. An Index of lack of social functioning was therefore developed for this purpose by CI staff.[1] In this paper it is referred to as the Social Functioning Index.

Since the patients at CI and the LC were not assigned those treatments from a common pool, a description of who they are and how they came to be there is important to the evaluation. The patients at the LC were a chronic schizophrenic population. All were physically healthy males between the ages of 20 and 48. They had exhibited high ratings on the MMPI schizophrenia scale 8 and had been diagnosed schizophrenic by two independent psychiatrists on the basis of interviews and observations revealing the following: (a) major thought disorder, (b) bizarre delusions with persecutory content, (c) auditory hallucinations, (d) flat and inappropriate affect, and (e) disorganized behavior in the face of clear sensorium and appropriate spatial orientation. EEG's revealed no evidence of focal neurological disorders. Routine blood chemistries were normal, and there was no history of known metabolic or other physical disorder. The patients had been hospitalized for at least four years and were unmedicated because they demonstrated no improvement with currently available antipsychotic drugs. The control subjects at the LC were also exclusively male.

The Cathexis School Program was a laboratory teaching program associated with Cathexis Institute, a non-profit organization devoted to research and training in the effective care of severe emotional disturbances. The organization was established in 1971 by Jacqui Lee Schiff, an early member of the San Francisco Social Psychiatry Seminar and one of the early contributors to transactional analysis. It was preceded by the Schiff Rehabilitation Project in which the concept of reparenting was developed (J. L. Schiff 1969). Eric Berne was a frequent visitor and consultant while this work was being done. The Passivity research which was published in the TAJ #1 is also very relevant to the program discussed here (A. Schiff and J. L. Schiff 1971). Transactional analysis and Reparenting were used continuously in conducting the programs and provided the theoretical framework for treatment and also molded the conceptual orientation of the community of therapists and subjects.

The program was a voluntary outpatient structure providing didactic and experiential classes for at least 2½ hours each weekday, a weekly treatment group, and other activities up to as much as ten additional hours of regularly structured time (including some activities on weekends). The program was designed to address many areas of information, provide a social structure based on transactional analysis, and give attention to each subject developing social skills. Group and community dynamics were used to support each individual throughout treatment.

The utilization of passivity confrontation was emphasized as an important part of the treatment structure. Each subject had a contract to confront from a caring position and to respond appropriately to confrontation from others. Passivity confrontation helped subjects by demanding that they identify problems and implement a relevant plan to address each problem. For subjects whose definitions of reality were tenuous, passivity confrontation was an acknowledged tool which many came to use enthusiastically and with confidence. It is, perhaps, important that it was considered a general responsibility by both staff and subjects to be certain that confrontation wasn't misused.

Part of the treatment philosphy required frequent change in the structure of the program in order to interrupt ongoing games. Also many subjects had difficulty adapting to change and this provides an opportunity to address that problem. Despite the programmed changes, the underlying educative model remained constant.

Subjects were encouraged to form meaningful relationships with members of the CI staff modelled after parent-child relationships. This special attachment within the transference relationship was often formalized with "parenting contracts", in which the therapists formally assumed parental roles in relation to a particular patient. Those subjects with parenting contracts were encouraged to decathect their Parent ego states and incorporate Parent from the contract parents (J. L. Schiff 1969) while their process was carefully monitored by the rest of the staff.

A treatment team consisted of approximately ten staff members chosen from various professional backgrounds. There was always a psychiatrist, a psychologist, a social worker, and an educator. In addition, there generally were trainees and interns. The staff met over dinner for three or more hours weekly. Generally, subjects were invited to attend these meetings. Additionally, staff met weekly in a treatment group for support, confrontation, and whatever personal work was needed. Working within transference relationships was seen as very difficult and stressful and it was considered by all those involved that this support was essential. Eric Berne stated that the most powerful transaction was the transference transaction. Very active support and supervision was seen as necessary for staff to work effectively within the transference relationship with a very disturbed and high-risk population.

This research does not distinguish those patients who were reparenting from those who were not. That is because those subjects who had parenting contracts sometimes did not follow through on them in a productive way, and some subjects who did not have parenting contracts formed very intense transference relationships with staff members. The subjects who did decathect Parent were generally those who did the best in treatment. The quality of relating can best be derived from the Index of Social functioning.

Frequently subjects were involved in the personal life and family activities of members of the staff as part of their participation in the program. Also, many activities such as social events, volunteer work within the organization, fund raising, and group participation in community outings, were encouraged and expected. Eventually subjects were guided into and through participation in social and educational activities outside the program. The classes were structured to provide new information and to correct misinformation, and invited subjects' active participation. The program also focused on active skill development, like cooking and money management, and theoretical instructions based on transactional analysis. The focus was continuously to help the subjects develop thinking processes which would enable and encourage them to develop skills in problem-solving and focus on a goal of becoming responsible and caring participants in the larger society. There was a great deal of emphasis on each person becoming a contributor in those situations in which he/she chose to be involved.

It was required that subjects live in approved housing. This might be special care homes for mentally disturbed individuals. Occasionally a subject was hospitalized briefly and continued in the program. As subjects improved, they were encouraged to move into cooperative housing with other subjects at approxiately the same stage of treatment. Later they were encouraged to live in cooperative housing with housemates who were not in treatment. When subjects were in special care homes, staff of Cathexis Institute was available to the caretakers in these homes for consultation and support. Also, some subjects lived for varying lengths of time in the homes of different staff members. Staff were always available for consultation by telephone.

Usually the program met later in the afternoon to accommodate subjects who were working or attending school and who were relatively advanced in treatment. Typically the program would offer several possibilities. A subject who displayed special problems might be expected to attend certain classes relevant to that problem. On any particular day the program might begin with a community meeting and announcements. Then the schedule for the first hour might include: (1) a seminar on paranoia, (2) a class on letter-writing, (3) a regressive lab, and (4) a class on daily problem-solving. The second hour, after a brief break, might include: (1) a TA 101 course, (2) a class for subjects who were new in the program, (3) a psychodrama activity, and (4) another class on daily problem-solving.

At other times during the day subjects might come in for activities ranging from individual counseling to an exercise class. However, it should be remembered that the program changed frequently.

Regressive activity was a very important part of the program for many subjects. Usually the patient would contract to be a certain age and to address a particular problem at that age. Sometimes regressive groups were organized around cultural activities considered to be a normal part of children's experiences, such as a trip to the zoo. Regressive work, involving full cathexis to child, often referred to as *"re-childing"* among transactional analysts, is essential in working with severely disturbed individuals for doing script work. It also provides treatment for the stroking and feeding issues which are among the problems subjects with psychoses present. It was believed by staff that the emphasis on regressive work very much reduced the likelihood of transference problems. As the subject became more able to function, the staff encouraged more autonomy and more mature participation in the program. The development of leadership traits was encouraged and rescripting became an important focus of treatment. Eventually the subject "graduated" from treatment. However, contracts around relatedness made during the course of treatment could be maintained so the subject experienced no loss or rejection as a consequence of getting well.

The above description of the program is not meant to substitute for training in the specifics of reparenting. Some therapists trying to develop their own programs have had unfortunate experiences either for themselves or the patient. It is necessary to remember that psychotic patients are dealing with third degree (life threatening) issues, and these from a specific (but understandable) frame of reference. CI can provide referals to qualified transactional analysis trainers.

Additionally, the treatment of psychosis is

very demanding and stressful for the therapist and may involve issues of protection which make it advisable that such treatment be undertaken only in a treatment structure with a fully qualified treatment team.

All participants in the School Program at CI were required to have a physical examination within six months of entering the program. Because of the nature of the program, people with injuries or diseases which would limit physical activities or exhibited significant evidence of neurological disorders were not deemed suitable for the program, and therefore would not become subjects in the experimental group.

The experimental group consisted of 20 males and 35 females ranging in age from 18 to 43. All subjects were participants in the CI School Program during the period of 1976 through 1979, except two subjects who were former participants and were included in the evaluation at the beginning of the period only and met the same criteria as the participants at that time. All the subjects in the experimental group were unmedicated since the program was structured to operate without the use of antipsychotic drugs.

The Biochemical Design

The quest for a biochemical basis of schizophrenia has led researchers down many different avenues. Much research has focused upon the role of the neurotransmitter dopamine because of the recognized dopaminergic inhibition produced by the major antipsychotic medications (Carlsson, 1976; Stein and Wise, 1971). Others, noting the relative lack of reward learning in schizophrenia have turned their attention to the opioid peptides such as β-endorphin (Goldblum, 1984). The resemblance of many hallucinogens to the neurotransmitter serotonin has given rise to investigation of serotinergic mechanisms in schizophrenia. A thorough review of such research can be found in the reports from a workshop on the biology of schizophrenia (DeLisi, et al., 1981).

Recognizing the diversity of opinion regarding the significance of any particular biochemical anomaly observed in schizophrenia, this study focuses upon the observation of a peculiarity in serotinergic metabolism as reflected by elevated transport of tryptophan into erythrocytes. This choice was made for several reasons. First, the chronic schizophrenic population at the LC, where this study was being conducted, repeatedly demonstrated an elevation in this measurement. Second, as interesting as the possible role of the endorphins might be, there is no simple blood test for examining this variable. Third, many of the patients being observed have not shown improvement with the standard antipsychotic medications. This is in keeping with reports that these drugs appear to ameliorate only the "positive" symptoms of the illness (delusions, hallucinations and thought disorder). "Negative" symptoms (flattening of affect, poverty of speech and loss of drive) commonly seen in chronic schizophrenia appear to be much less affected by these dopaminergic inhibitors (Johnstone, et al. 1978). Observation of variables other than those reflecting dopaminergic metabolism might be fruitful for this particular group of schizophrenics. It has been suggested that "negative" symptoms appear related to ventricular enlargement in the brain (Andreasen, 1981), which in turn correlates with abnormalities in serotonin metabolism observed in erythrocytes (Stahl, et al. 1982). Finally, observations of peripheral serotonin metabolism have repeatedly revealed abnormalities in patient groups similar to those studied (Andreasen, 1981, Stahl, et al. 1982, Todrich, et al. 1960, Garelis, et al. 1975, Joseph, et al. 1977, Freedman, et al. 1981). This suggests that these elevations in serotonin may reflect an increased tryptophan uptake in chronic undifferentiated schizophrenics. The assay used in this study measures tryptophan uptake.

The measurement of the amount of radioactive tryptophan which is present inside chicken erythrocytes following incubation in a medium containing C-14 tryptophan along with human plasma is referred to in the literature as "tryptophan uptake" (Frohman, et al. 1969). It is used as an indicator of the degree of activity of a serum protein factor which affects the mechamisms which regulate transport of tryptophan across cell membranes. It first became associated with the study of schizophrenia following the observation that serum from schizophrenic patients, when injected into rats inhibited reward learning but not avoidance learning. Serum from control subjects did not have this effect. It was determined that the substance responsible for this was a protein (an *a*-2 globulin) which, among other things, altered the transport of tryptophan across chicken erythrocyte membranes. Measurement of "tryptophan uptake" was developed by Charles Frohman (1969) and his co-workers at the LC into a quantitative assay for the presence of that protein. Gottleib. et al. (1970) found that about 60% of the schizophrenics studied exhibited elevated tryptophan uptake.[2]

Originally it was thought that tryptophan uptake was reflecting the presence of some sort of abnormal substance produced in the bodies of schizophrenics. As studies continued it became clear that under certain conditions of stress, plasma from normal control subjects could similarly affect tryptophan uptake determination, although to a lesser extent than that of the schizophrenics.

This observation led to the current view that the *a*-2 globulin, whose activity is reflected in tryptophan uptake, is a normal part of a feedback controlled system which allows tryptophan transport into the brain to be responsive to external conditions such as stress. In schizophrenia the set point for this system is abnormally high, at least in the early stages of the illness. Researchers at LC have isolated a second protein referred to as the "anti-factor" which when added to plasma from schizophrenics reduces the tryptophan uptake measurement (Gottleib, et al. 1970).

Tryptophan transport into brain cells, which behave like chicken erythrocytes in this regard, is of interest in the study of schizophrenia becase tryptophan is converted in the brain to serotonin. Serotronin is an important neurotransmitter in diverse brain centers and can influence basic drives (hunger, thirst, sleep, etc.), perception of pain, affective responses, thinking, and regulation of hormones. Some of its metabolites are also hallucinogens, so it is theoretically possible that increased tryptophan uptake could ultimately result in autoproduction of hallucinogenic compounds.

Procedure

Evaluations were done on CI patients on all three indices near the time of intake. Subsequent evaluations were done at approximately six month intervals, midwinter and summer. Some individuals were followed throughout the duration of the research; others left the program and were included for shorter periods of time. (See Table 4.)

At the time of each testing the first 400 questions on the MMPI were administered, and the 78 items comprising scale #8, (the schizophrenic scale) were used. The test is scored so that higher scores indicate a higher level of schizophrenic symptoms.

Patients were scored on the Social Functioning Scale jointly by staff and the individual being evaluated, sometimes in consultation with others familiar with the subject's behaviour in living or social situations. Scores ranged from 10 to 0 with those who were the most dysfunctional scoring highest.

Triptophan uptake was measured as previously described using chicken erythrocytes which were placed in an incubating medium containing plasma from the patients at CI. Plasma was placed on ice and flown from Oakland to Detroit immediately after it was drawn and the assays were performed as soon as samples were received. Assays were always performed using at least one sample of control plasma.

Tryptophan uptake determinations were performed on plasma which had been drawn from schizophrenic and control subjects at the LC at 8:00AM on the day of the assay. The technicians who did the assays were blind as to condition, and at least two of the three groups were always assayed at the same time.

Results

A preliminary analysis was performed comparing the tryptophan uptake readings on the patients and controls at the LC. The median reading for each patient and each control was calculated. The probability that a randomly selected control has a higher median tryptophan uptake than a randomly selected patient was estimated to be 4%, which justifies using tryptophan uptake as one measure of schizophrenic illness. Additionally a hint was found that tryptophan uptake is higher in the winter than in the summer, a matter further explored below.

The Regression Model

Much of the analysis rests on a basic regression equation model described here. The dependent variable is transformed tryptophan uptake, $y = 2 - (2/\ Z)$, where Z is measured tryptophan uptake. This transformation, a member of the Box-Cox (1964) family of transformations, is chosen to straighten the residual plots of the regressions described below. Below this transformed variable is referred to as tryptophan uptake. The independent variables used in these regressions were duration of treatment (measured for LC patients and controls by the number of months since first tryptophan uptake measurement, and for CI patients by the number of months actually in treatment), a constant for each person, and a trigonometric form explained below.

As mentioned above, a preliminary analysis

indicated that tryptophan uptake measurements might be influenced by some sort of seasonal biological oscillation resulting in higher readings in the winter than in the summer. In order to avoid having the analysis contaminated by this factor, and also to measure its magnitude, an additive term is included in the analysis describing such a periodic variation,

$$y \cos \lambda (t-ø) \qquad (1)$$

Since t is measured in months and a yearly cycle is suspected, λ is taken to be $2\pi/12 = \pi/6$. Here the parameter λ indicates how large the fitted cycle is, while ø indicates the time of year in months when the peak occurs. In particular, ø = 0 indicates a peak at December 1, while ø = 6 indicates a peak on June 1. Thus the form (1) allows for a yearly cycle of arbitrary amplitude y and phase ø. See Appendix A.

The full model used in the analysis below can be written

$$Y_{it} = y \cos(\lambda(t-\text{ø})) + \delta_i + \eta d_{it} + \varepsilon_{it} \qquad (2)$$

where Y_{it} is the value of the dependent variable (tryptophan uptake) for persion i (patient or control) at time t, δ is a constant allowed to be different for each person i, d_{it} is the duration of treatment (as defined above) for each person i at each time t, ε_{it} is an independent normally distributed error term with zero mean and variance σ. Finally y, ø, η, δ_i, and σ^2 are parameters to be estimated.

Such a model is useful because it allows the simultaneous estimation of all of the parameters of the system: those governing the yearly cyclic behaviour (y and ø), that governing duration (η), the individual constants (δ), and the variance σ^2. An alternative, sequential treatment would have opened the possibility that the estimated effects would depend on the order in which the estimation steps were conducted.

It might be supposed that, as a function of time since onset, or time since treatment began, tryptophan uptake of a schizophrenic declines at a constant rate to the normal level. Since when onset was for each patient, or when to count treatment as having begun is not known, this is taken into account by allowing a separate constant for each patient, as estimated above.

Results of the Model for Tryptophan Uptake: Staff v. Hospitalized Patients

The first results to examine use LC tryptophan uptake as dependent variable and are summarized in Table 1. In that Table, the "median constant" column reports the median of the δ_i, and the standard error of the median constant reports the median of the standard errors of the $\hat{\delta}_i$. Giving the results in this form avoids unnecessary detail (16 patient constants and 15 staff constants, respectively), but still gives an idea of how large the numbers tend to be.

Table 1

Regression Results: LC Tryptophan Uptake

Description of Tryptophan Uptake

Dependent Variable: LC Patient Tryptophan Uptake
Independent Variables: Duration Patient Constants, Cosine Function

		Estimate	St. Error of Estimate
Coefficient of Duration	(η)	-.0006/mo.	.001/mo.
Median Constant	(median $\hat{\delta}$)	.890	.057*
Amplitude	y	.062	.035
Phase	(ø)	.231 (Dec. 7)	1.21/m

Indicators of the reliability of the regression

Standard Error (σ)	2.60 units of tryptophan uptake
Multiple R^2	.193

Number of persons = 16 Number of observations = 403

*This is the median of the standard errors of the estimates $\hat{\delta}_i$

cont.......

..... table 1 cont....

Dependent Variable: LC Control of Tryptophan Uptake
Independent Variables: Duration, Control Constants, Cosine Funtion

		Estimate	St. Error of Estimate
Coefficient of Duration	(η)	-.0003/mo.	.001/mo.
Median Cosntant	(median $\hat{\delta}$)	.605	.076*
Amplitude	y	.048	.029
Phase	(ø)	-.754 (Nov. 8)	1.01/mo.

Standard Error (σ)	2.71 units of tryptophan uptake
Multiple R^2	.297

Number of persons = 15 Number of observations = 225

*This is the median of the standard errors of the estimates $\hat{\delta}_i$

Table 2

Regression Results: LC Tryptophan Uptake Without Duration

Description of Tryptophan Uptake

Dependent Variable: LC Patient Tryptophan Uptake
Independent Variables: Patient Constants, Cosine Function

		Estimate	St. Error of Estimate
Median Constant	(median $\hat{\delta}$)	.871	.054*
Amplitude	y	.068	.037
Phase	ø	.055 (Dec. 2)	.978/mo.

Indicators of the reliability of the regression

Standard Error (σ)	.260 units of tryptophan uptake
Multiple R^2	.192

Number of persons = 16 Number of observations = 403

*This is the median of the standard errors of the estimates $\hat{\delta}_i$

cont....

....table 2 cont....

Depedent Variable: LC Patient Tryptophan Uptake
Independent Variables: Control Constants, Cosine Function

		Estimate	St. Error of Estimate
Median Constant	(median $\hat{\delta}$)	.611	.070*
Amplitude	y	.050	.028
Phase	(ø)	-.825 (Nov. 6)	.942/mo.

Indicators of the reliability of the regression

Standard Error (σ)	2.70 units of tryptophan uptake
Multiple R^2	.297

Number of persons = 15 Number of observations = 225

*This is the median of the standard errors of the estimates $\hat{\delta}_i$

The weakness of the duration variable leads to consideration of the possibility of dropping it as a variable from the regression. If duration does not matter, then both groups would be regarded as constant over time. Table 2 records the results, which are quite comparable to those in Table 1. The duration constants are so small in Table 1 that Table 2's results are taken as the best representation of both sets of LC Data.

Cathexis Institute Patients

The same regression equation model applied to the 55 CI patients for whom tryptophan uptake readings are available yields the results reported in Table 3. The phase of the cycle is comparable to that of the LC patients and controls; its amplitude is closer to that of the controls. The median constant is comparable to that of the LC patients, which suggests that LC patients and CI patients had, at the beginning of the experiment, roughly comparable tryptophan uptake levels. However, the coefficient of the duration variable is substantially different. Since $-.8 \times 10^{-2}$ units of tryptophan uptake per month is not an easy number to

Table 3

Regression Results: CI Tryptophan Uptake

Description of the Tryptophan Uptake

Dependent Variable: LC Patient Tryptophan Uptake
Independent Variables: Patient Constants, Cosine Function, Duration

		Estimate	St. Error of Estimate
Coefficient of Duration	(η)	-.008/mo.	.001/mo.
Median Constant	(median ($\hat{\delta}$)	.934	.097*
Amplitude	y	.052	.029
Phase	(ø)	1.941 (Jan. 29)	.835/mo.

Indicators of the reliability of the regression

Standard Error (σ)	.211 units of tryptophan uptake
Multiple R^2	.402

Number of persons = 55 Number of observations = 400

*This is the median of the standard errors of the estimates $\hat{\delta}_i$

appreciate, the number of months of CI treatment it would require for the tryptophan uptake level of a CI patient starting with a tryptophan uptake level equal to that of the median LC patients, to drop to the level of the median LC control is calculated, if such an extrapolation were valid. The legitimacy of such an extrapolation is not claimed. It is used merely to clarify the implications of the coefficient of duration. This calculation yields 32.7 months. Uncertainty in the duration effects produces a standard error of 5.4 months. Thus the two-standard-deviation interval for this number is from almost two years to about three and one-half years.

This calculation should not be overinterpreted. Certainly the populations of patients are potentially different. Diagnostic systems are not so precise that schizophrenics at one institution are certain to be the same as those at another.[3] Nor need the severity of illness of patients at the LC be regarded as the same as those who volunteered for outpatient treatment at the CI in Oakland. Had this calculation suggested such improvement in ten years, this would have been discouraging. Had it been as short as three months, say, it would be too brief to be believable short of miracles. Staff at CI predicted that successful treatment of schizophrenia is likely to take approximately five years.

To assess the reliability of the estimate of 32.7 months as described above, it is important to see whether or not the estimate is an extrapolation beyond the range of the available data. Table 4 contains information on the length of time over which data were collected from CI patients.

Table 4

Distribution of Time since First Tryptophan Uptake Reading of CI Patients

Number of Months	0-4	5-9	10-14	15-19
Last Reading on a patient	20	8	5	6
All Readings	168	66	48	52

Number of Months	20-24	25-29	30-34	35-up
Last Reading[1]	3	3	6	4
All Readings[2]	22	16	17	11

1 The number of patient readings falling in the time interval.

2 The number in the table is the number of patients whose last reading falls in the time interval.

For each patient, the number of months of CI treatment which elapsed between the first tryptophan uptake reading on that patient and the last one were calculated. The results are reported in line 1 of Table 4. For each patient, and for each tryptophan uptake reading after the first one on that patient, the number of months of CI treatment that elapsed between that reading and the first reading for that patient were also calculated. These results are reported in line 2 of Table 4. Out of 55 patients, four (or 7%) had over 32.7 months of CI treatment between their first and last tryptophan uptake reading. Furthermore, 11 out of 400 readings were taken at over 32.7 months after the first reading for the patient. This represents about three percent of the tryptophan uptake readings. Thus, 32.7 months is just barely within the range of the available data.[4]

A second possible interpretation of these regression results is the level of tryptophan uptake declines in hyperbolic fashion after onset of schizophrenia. Under this interpretation, the CI patients are observed sooner after onset than the LC patients, and this accounts for the faster decline of tryptophan uptake observed among the CI patients. This hypothesis cannot be checked against the data directly, since time of "onset" is not well-defined and no attempt was made to measure it in this study. However, observe that the median constant for the LC patients is about .87 (see Table 2), and for the CI patients the median constant is .93 (from Table 3). These numbers are much closer together than either is to .61, the median constant of the LC staff. This suggests that the two sets of patients were at roughly the same level of tryptophan uptake at the times they entered the study, which was taken as t=0 in both models. And this observation is inconsistent with the hyperbolic model.

Since higher levels of tryptophan uptake appear to be associated with schizophrenia, a drop in those levels associated with a treatment program is heartening. It cannot be regarded as conclusive, however, since tryptophan uptake may drop for other reasons. One can look, then, to the MMPI test and the index of social functioning for possible corroborating evidence of improvement.

It is reasonable to suppose that the MMPI Scale 8 measurements of untreated schizophrenia do not change over time. While directly corroborating or contradictory articles were not found, longitudinal studies of schizophrenic population using Scale 8 with elapsed time shorter than one year (Carp 1950, Hales and Simon 1948, Pacella, Piotrowski and Lewis 1947, and Simon, et al. 1958) and longitudinal studies of mixed or non-schizophrenic populations using Scale 8 was found (Barron and Leary

1955, Johnson and McNeal 1965, Jurjevich 1966, Kaufmann 1950, Lewinsohn 1965, Lewinsohn and Nichols 1964, Mariger 1972, Schofield 1950, 1953 Sines, Silver and Lucero 1961, and Stone 1965). Perhaps the most closely related studies are by May (1968) and Rogers (1967), both of which use Scale 8 to assess the effectiveness of treatments for schizophrenia.

Both the MMPI Scale 8 and the Index of Social Functioning are arranged so that higher scores indicate higher levels of schizophrenic symptoms. For these latter two scales only summer and winter readings are available. The regression equation model is consequently modified slightly, to have a dummy variable for winter in place of the cosine function (1).

Table 5

Cathexis Institute MMPIs

Description of MMPI Results

CI Patient MMPIs

Independent Variables: Duration, Season, Personal Constants

		Estimate	St. Error of Estimates
Coefficient of Duration	(η)	.59/mo.	.12/mo.
Median Constant	(median $\hat{\delta}_i$)	104.23	9.03*
Season		-2.14	2.16

Indicators of the reliability of the regression

Standard Error (σ)	13.70 MMPI units
Multiple R^2	.98

Number of persons = 52 Number of observations = 183

*This is the median of the standard errors of the estimates $\hat{\delta}_i$

Table 6

Social Index Results

Description of Social Index

Dependent Variable: CI Patient Index of Social Functioning
Independent Variables: Duration, Season, Personal Constants

		Estimate	St. Error of Estimate
Coefficient of Duration	(η)	-.0683/mo.	.011/mo.
Median Constant	(median $\hat{\delta}$)	6.470	.868*
Season		-.383	.209

Indicators of the reliability of the regression

Standard Error (σ)	1.27 Social Index units
Multiple R^2	.95

Number of persons = 53 Number of observations = 174

*This is the median of the standard errors of the estimates $\hat{\delta}_i$

The results are given in Tables 5 and 6. In both cases the duration coefficients are negative, indicating improvement associated with length of treatment in CI. In the hypothetical 32.7 months of treatment previously discussed, a CI patient's MMPI would decline 19.3 points (standard error 4.0) and the social index 2.2 (standard error .36). The season coefficients are relatively less well estimated, but both have negative signs, indicating, if anything, a lower level of schizophrenic symptoms associated with the winter months, which is contrary to our findings with respect to tryptophan uptake.

While unfortunately MMPI and Social Functioning Index Scores for the LC patients are not available, the results here do confirm the impression from Table 3 of improvement in CI patients during treatment.

Findings

1. The LC data confirms that tryptophan uptake is characteristically higher for schizophrenics than for others.

2. In both the LC data and the CI data there is evidence of a yearly cycle in tryptophan uptake with the peak roughly in late fall or early winter.

3. The LC control and patient populations appear to be otherwise static in time with respect to tryptophan uptake.

4. The CI population's level of tryptophan uptake declines over time at the rate of approximately 0.8×10^{-2} units of tryptophan uptake per month.

5. Analysis of the MMPI and Social Index Data of the CI population shows similar corroborating improvement over time.

6. The MMPI and Social Indices show, if anything, cyclic behavior opposite to that of all three groups with respect to tryptophan uptake.

Discussion

The finding of the yearly cycle in tryptophan uptake is intriguing. Several possible explanations might be given. Because tryptophan uptake is determined by means of a bioassay, it is possible that the cycles are an artifact of seasonal changes in the condition of the chicken erythrocytes used in the assay. Another more interesting possibility is that the cycle reflects an actual seasonal cycle for the system regulating tryptophan uptake. This is not unlikely since one of the brain areas where tryptophan uptake is especially important, the pineal body, is known to produce melatonin from tryptophan in amounts which vary seasonally. The pineal is also a rich source of the "antifactor" previously mentioned. Yet another possibility is that it might reflect greater excitement around Christmas time, or it might reflect some kind of internal bodily rhythm. Comparison data from a country with a similar cultural emphasis on a December holiday from well south of the equator (where presumably yearly internal bodily rhythms would be reversed) might be a way to distinguish between the second and third hypotheses.

The import of the changes in MMPI results and social functioning is not clear. By the time the tryptophan uptake reading would extrapolate to normal, the MMPI would be extrapolated to drop from a median of 104 to a median of 85, still a high value on the schizophrenia scale. However, clinicians at the CI regard this level of improvement as important because it makes the patients more available to treatment. The Social Functioning Index scale would go from 6.5 to 4.3, meaning that on the average roughly two of the ten problems listed in Footnote 1 would have been solved during this period.

Some of the drop in tryptophan uptake among the CI patients could be ascribed to the mechanisms causing the slow drop (6×10^{-4}/month) observed among the LC patients. If that were the primary cause, however, we would not expect to see a drop as fast as we observe (8×10^{-3}/month), and we would not expect to see improvement in the MMPI or in the social functioning index. When all of this is taken together, it suggests that patients being treated at CI do exhibit some degree of improvement without the use of drugs. Because these patients initially exhibited evidence of biochemical abnormality, it is interesting that biochemical intervention (i.e. drugs) were not needed to bring about such improvement. It suggests that, given the known side effects of the antipsychotic medications, further development and testing of techniques such as those used at CI would be worthwhile. (See also Fairweather (1964), Mosher and Menn (1978), Flomenhaft, Kaplan and Langsley (1969), Brook (1973), and Stein, Test and Marx (1975)).

The findings reported here, that patients in Cathexsis treatment improve more rapidly with respect to tryptophan uptake than do research subjects at the LC, are broadly consistent with the secondary analysis literature (see Braun, Kochansky, Shapiro, Greenberg, Grudeman, Johnson and Shore (1981), Greene and De la Cruz (1981), Kiesler (1982, 1983), Smith et al. (1980), and Straw (1982). Those studies find, in the main, greater effectiveness for a variety of alternative treatment regimes compared to hospitalization, using various dependent measures.

REFERENCES

Anastasi, A. (1976). *Psychological Testing, 4.* New York: MacMillan.

Breasen, N. (1981, July). *Ct scan abnormalities in schizophrenia: Relationship to positive & negative symptoms.* Paper presented at the annual meeting of the Royal College of Psychiatrists Annual Meeting, London, England.

Barron, F. & Leary, T. F. (1955). Changes in psychoneurotic patients with & without psychotherapy, *Journal of Consulting Psychology, 19* 239-45.

Bishop, M. P. (1963). Effects of Plasma from Schizophrenic Subjects Upon Learning & Retention in the Rat, in R. G. Heath (Ed.), *Serological Fractions in Schizophrenia.* New York: Harper & Row.

Bishop, Y., Fienberg, S. & Holland, P. (1975). *Discrete Multivariate Analysis: Theory and Practice,* Cambridge: MIT Press.

Box, G. E. P. & Cox, D. R. (1964). An Analysis of Transformations. *Journal of the Royal Statistical Society*, Series B, *26*, 211-252.

Braun, P., Kochansky, G., Shapiro, R., Greenberg, S., Gudeman, J. E., Johnson, S. & Shore, M. F. (1981). Overview: Deinstitutionalization of psychiatric patients, a critical review of outcome studies. *American Journal of Psychiatry*, *138*, 736-749.

Brook, B. D. (1973). An alternative to psychiatric hospitalization for emergency patients. *Hospital & Community Psychiatry*, *24*, 621-624.

Carlsson, A. (1976). Impact of pharmacology on the problem of Schizophrenia. In D. Kemali, G. Bartholini & D. Richter (Ed.), *Schizophrenia Today* (pp. 89-103). Oxford: Pergammon Press.

Carp, Abraham, (1950). MMPI Performance & Insulin Shock Therapy. *Journal of Abnormal & Social Psychology*, *45*, 721-26.

DeLisi, L. E., Neckers, L. H., Heinberger, D. R., et al. (1981). Elevated blood serotonin concentrations in unmedicated chronic schizophrenic patients. *Archives of General Psychiatry*, *38*, 647-650.

Dohrenwend, B. P., Dohrenwend, B. S., Gould, M. S., Link, B., Neugebauer, R. & Wunsh-Hitzig, R. (1980). *Mental Illness in the United States: Epidemiological Estimates*. New York: Praeger.

Eicker, F. (1963). Asymptotic Normality & Consistency of the Least Squares Estimators for Families of Linear Regressions. *Annals of Mathematical Statistics, 34,* 447-456.

Fairweather, G. W. (1964). *Social Psychology in Treating Mental Illness*. New York: Wiley.

Flomenhaft, K., Kaplan, D. M. & Langsley, D. G. (1969). Avoiding psychiatric hospitalization. *Social Work, 16,* 38-45.

Fraser, D. A. S. (1957). *Nonparametric Methods in Statistics*. New York: Wiley.

Freedman, D. X., Belendiuk, K., Belendiuk, G. H., et al. (1981). Blood tryptophan metabolism in chronic schizophrenic patients, *Archives of General Psychiatry, 38,* 647-658.

Frohman, C. E., Warner, K. A., Yoon, H. S., Arthur, R. E. & Gotlieb, J. S. (1969). The Plasma Factor & Transport of Indoleamine Acids, *Biological Psychiatry 1.*

Garelis, E., Gillin, J. C., Hyath. R. J., et al. (1975). Elevated blood serotonin concentrations in unmedicated chronic schizophrenic patients, a preliminary study, *American Journal of Psychiatrics, 132,* 184-186.

Goldblum, D. S. (1984, June) Endogenous Opiates & Schizophrenia: Directions in Clinical Research, *Canadian Journal of Psychiatry 29,* (4), 355-60.

Gottlieb, Jacques, S., Frohman, Charles E., & Beckett, P. G. S. (1970). The Current Status of the *a*-2-Globulin in Schizophrenia. In H. E. Himwich (Ed.) *Biochemistry, Schizophrenias & Affective Illnesses* (pp. 153-170). Baltimore: Williams & Wilkins Co.

Graybill, F. (1976). *Theory & Application of the Linear Model.* North Scituate: Duxbury Press.

Green, L. R. & De La Cruz (1981, Fall). A Psychiatric treatment, an alternative to & transition from full-time hospitalization, *Community, Mental Health Journal, 17,* 17, 191-202.

Hales, William M. & Simon, Werner (1948). Patterns before & after insulin shock therapy, *American Journal of Psychiatry, 105,* 254-8.

Hendrie, H. C., Ward, V. L. & Erb. J. C. (1969). C-Labelled Tryptophan Uptake & Anxiety, *Biological Psychiatry,* 14, 221.

Himwich, H. E. (1970). Indoleamines & the Schizophrenias. In H. E. Himwich (Ed.). *Biochemistry, Schizophrenias & Affective Illnesses.* (pp. 79-122). Baltimore: Williams & Wilkins Co.

Johnston, Roy & McNeal, Benjamin (1965). Residual psychopathology in released psychiatric patients & its relation to readmission. *Journal of Abnormal Psychology, 70,* 337-42.

Johnstone, E. C., Crow, T. J., Frith, C. D., Carney, M. W. P. & Price, J. S. (1978, April). Mechanisms of the antipsychotic effect in the treatment of acute schizophrenia, *Lancet 1* (8069), 848-851.

Joseph, M. H., Owen, F., Baker, H. F., et al. (1977). Platelet serotonin concentration & monoamine oxidaze activity in unmedicated chronic schizophrenic & schizoaffective patients, *Psychological Medicine 7,* 159-162.

Jurjevich, R. M. (1966). Short-interval test-retest stability of MMPI, California Psychological Inventory, Cornell Index & Symptoms Checklist, *Journal of General Psychology, 74,* 201-06.

Kaufmann, P. (1950). Changes in the MMPI as a function of psychiatric therapy. *Journal of Consulting Psychology,* 14, 458-64.

Kjesler, C. A. (1982). Mental Hospitals & alternative care: Non-institutionalization as potential public policy for mental patients. *American Psychologist, 37,* 349-360.

Keisler, C. A. (1983). Public & Professional Myths about Mental Hospitalization: An Emperical Reassessment of Policy-Related Beliefs, *American Psychologist, 37,* 1323-1330.

Lewinsohn, P. (1965). Dimensions of MMPI Change, *Journal of Clincal Psychology, 21,* 37-43.

Lewinsohn, P. M. & Nichols, R. C. (1964). The evaluation of changes in psychiatric patients during & after hospitalization. *Journal of Clinical Psychology, 20,* 272-9.

Lozovsky, D., Krasnova, A., Factor, M., Polyanskaya, N. & Popova, N. (1967). The effect of the serum of schizophrenic patients upon certain glucose transformations. *Transactions of the Symposium on Biologic Research in Schizophrenia, 151.* Moscow: Lenin Printing Co.

Mariger, P. (1972). The test-retest reliability of persons: an empirical investigation utilizing the MMPI & the personality research form, (Doctoral Dissertation, University of Minnesota, 1972), *Dissertation Abstracts International, 33,* 2816B.

May, P. R. A. (1968). (Ed.) *Treatment in Schizophrenia: a comparative study of five treatment methods.* New York: Science House.

Mosher, L. R. & Menn, A. Z. (1978). Community residential treatment for schizophrenia: Two year follow-up, *Hospital & Community Psychiatry, 29,* 715-723.

Nemeroff, C.B. & Bissette, G. Neuropeptides, Dolpamine, and Schizophrenia. *Annals of New York Acadamy of Science.* (5NM) 1988; 537: 273-291.

North, C.S., Current Concepts of Schizophrenia, *Comprehensive Practice of Therapy.* (DMZ) 1989, March, Vol.15 (3) 8-21.

Pacella, B. L., Piotrowski, Z. & Lewis, N. D. C. (1947). the Effects of Electric Convulsive Therapy on certain personality traits in psychiatric patients, *American Journal of Psychiatry, 104,* 83-91.

Pavlidis, T. (1973). *Biological Oscillators: Their Mathematical Analysis,* New York: Academic Press.

Rao, C. R. (1973). *Linear Statistical Inference & its Applications,* (2nd edition). New York: John Wiley.

Rogers, C. R. (1967). (Ed.) *The therapeutic relationship & its impact: a study of psychotherapy with schizophrenics.* Madison: University of Wisconsin Press.

Schiff, J. L. (1969). Reparenting Schizophrenics, *Transactional Analysis Bulletin 8, 31,* 47-63.

Schiff, A. W. & Schiff, J. L. (1971, July). Passivity, *Transactional Analysis Journal 1,* 71-78.

Schiff, J. L. (1975). *Cathexis Institute Reader,* New York: Harper & Row.

Schofield, W. (1950a). Changes in responses to the Minnesota Multiphasic Inventory following certain therapies, *Psychology & Monographs, 64,* (5, Seriel No. 311).

Schofield, W. (1950b). A further study of the effects of therapies on MMPI responses, *Journal of Abnormal & Social Psychology, 48:* 67-77.

Simon, W., Wirt, R. D., et al. (1958). A controlled study of the short-term differential treatment of schizophrenia, *American Journal of Psychiatry, 114,* 1077-85.
Sines, L. K., Silver, R. J. & Lucero, R. J. (1961). The effect of therapeutic intervention by untrained 'therapists', *Journal of Clinical Psychology, 17,* 394-6.

Smith, M. L. Glass, G. V. & Miller, T. I. (1980). The Benefits of Psychotherapy, Baltimore: The Johns Hopkins University Press.

Stahl, S. H. Ciaranello, R. D., Berger, P. H. (1982). Platelet serotonin in schizophrenia & depression: a review. In Ho B. T., Schoolar, J. C., Usdin, E. et al., (Eds.). *Serotonin in Biological Psychiatry: Advances in Biochemical Psychopharmacology, Vol. 34.* New York: Raven Press.

Stahl, S. H., Woo, D. M., Mefford, I. N. Berger, P. H. (1983). Hyperserotonemia & Platelet Serotonin Uptake & Release in Schizophrenia & Affective Disorders, *American Journal of Psychiatry 140, 1,* 26-30.

Stein, L. & C. D. Wise (1971) Possible Etiology of Schizophrenia *Science 171,* 1032.

Stein, L. I., Test, M. A. & Marx. A. J. (1975). Alternatives to the hospital: A controlled study, *American Journal of Psychiatry, 132,* 517-521.

Stone, L. A. (1965). Test-retest stability of the MMPI Scales, *Psychological Reports, 16,* 619-20.

Straw, R. B., (1982). *Meta-analysis of deinstitutionalization in mental health.* Unpublished Ph.D. dissertation, Northwestern University, Evanston, IL.

Todrich, A., Tai, A.C., Marshall, E.F., et al. (1960). Blood platelet 5HT levels in psychiatric patients, *British Journal of Psychiatry, 106,* 884-890.

Warner, K. A., Frohman, C. E. & Gotlieb, J. S. (1972). The effect of the plasma factor on the uptake of amino acids by neural tissues. *Biological Psychiatry, 5,* 23.

ACKNOWLEDGEMENTS

The authors thank Dr. Jerry Freidman of the Stanford Linear Accelerator for his hospitality, and for making his computer graphics system available during the Spring of 1979. Much of the data analysis was accomplished during a Seminar in Psychiatric Statistics taught by Kadane with help from Schervish during the Spring of 1980. We thank Avital Cnaan, Percival Darko and Sherryl May for their assistance in this connection. We also thank Professors Charles Kiesler and Jill Larkin for very helpful comments. The authors also express appreciation to the patients who participated in this study and also the very supportive staff at Cathexis Institute.

FOOTNOTES

1. The Index of Lack of Social Functioning consists of the following items:

(a) Demonstrates normal habit activities for self care (dress, eating, etc.); b) able to converse coherently; c) takes initiative to ask appropriately for things; d) contributes to up-keep of living situation (keeps room clean, helps with cooking, etc.); e) structures recreational activities independently; f) engages in normal heterosexual activity; g) able to manage money independently; h) maintains independent social relationships; i) able to maintain independent living and j) able to earn a living.

Score on the index is the number of items not true of the subject.

The item on the Index which refers to heterosexual relating does not refer specifically to sexual activity, but to the subject's being able to relate in a meaningful way at a social level to individuals of the opposite sex. For many subjects this was a behavior in which there were many problems derived from negative scripting or unhappy experiences with sex, and must necessarily be resolved as part of treatments.

2. Lozovsky et al. (1967) observed that a factor which may be the same as the factor influencing tryptophan uptake, has predictable patterns at different stages of the schizophrenic illness. For example, in the group they call "periodic schizophrenic" the highest level of the factor they measure occurs "during the first year after the onset of the disease, while afterward it kept growing lower, approaching the normal level by the 5th to 7th year" (p. 152).

3. Dohrenwend, Dohrenwend, Gould, Link, Neugebauer & Wunsch-Hitzig (1980) reported that incidence of mental diseases varies regionally. This could be partly due to regional differences in diagnostic practices. The implications of this for comparing schizophrenics at the LC with those at CI are unknown.

4. Another possible concern is serial correlation. Plots of residuals against previous residual for the same person revealed scant evidence of such correlations, so the independence model was used.

Appendix A

Expression of the Regression in Linear Form

The form (1) is awkward to put into a regression because it is non-linear in the parameter ϕ. Consequently the following transformation is used:

$$\gamma \cos \lambda\, (t-\phi) = \lambda \cos \lambda t \cos \lambda\phi + \gamma \sin \lambda t \sin \lambda\phi$$

Now let

$$\alpha = \gamma \sin \lambda\varphi \text{ and } \beta = \lambda \cos \gamma\phi$$

Then, solving, we obtain

$$\phi = (1/\lambda) \tan^{-1} (\alpha/\beta) = (6/\pi) \tan^{-1} (\alpha/\beta)$$

and $\gamma = \sqrt{\alpha^2 + \beta^2}$ (A1)

Thus instead of using (1) in the regression we equivalently use

$$\gamma \cos (t-\phi) = \alpha \sin \lambda t + \beta \cos \lambda. \qquad \text{(A2)}$$

which is a linear coefficients a and β, and then use (Al) to solve back for ϕ and γ. The method of regressing on the sine and cosine functions is discussed by Graybill[30].

From a linear regression using (A2) and other independent variables, estimates $\hat{\alpha}$ and $\hat{\beta}$ of α and β are found. It is natural, then, to use the estimates

$$\hat{\phi} = (6/\pi) \tan^{-1} (\hat{\alpha}/\hat{\beta}) \text{ and } \hat{\gamma} = \sqrt{\hat{\alpha}^2 + \hat{\beta}^2} \quad \text{(A3)}$$

for ϕ and γ. Transformation of the estimates requires a coincident transformation of the standard errors so that the reader may have some idea of how much sampling variability there is in the data. The full model can be written in the form

$$\begin{aligned} T_{ij} &= \gamma \cos \lambda (t-\phi) + \delta_i + \eta d_{it} + \varepsilon_{it} \\ &= \alpha \sin \lambda t + \beta \cos \lambda t + \delta_i + \eta d_{it} + \varepsilon_{ij} \end{aligned}$$

where

δ_i is a constant for each person i

d_{it} is the duration of treatment for persons i at time t

ε_{it} is a normally distributed error term, and
T_{ij} is the dependent variable

Let $\delta = (\delta_1, \ldots, \delta_n)$ be the vector of person-constants. When the sample size m is large, under standard regularity conditions[31] we have that,

$$\sqrt{m}\begin{pmatrix}\hat{\alpha}-\alpha\\ \hat{\beta}-\beta\\ \hat{\delta}-\delta\\ \hat{\eta}-\eta\end{pmatrix}$$ converges in distribution to a normal distribution with mean

0, and a covariance matrix Σ available from the computer output of a regression program. Then

$$\sqrt{m}\begin{pmatrix}\hat{\phi}-\phi\\ \hat{\gamma}-\gamma\\ \hat{\delta}-\delta\\ \hat{\eta}-\eta\end{pmatrix}$$ again converges to a normal distribution with mean 0, and

covariance matrix V, where V and Σ are related by the equality

$$V = A\,\Sigma\,A'$$

where

$$A = \frac{\partial\,(\phi, \gamma, \delta, \eta)}{\partial\,(\alpha, \beta, \delta, \eta)} = \begin{bmatrix} A_1 & 0 \\ 0 & I \end{bmatrix}, \text{ and}$$

$$A_1 = \begin{bmatrix} \frac{\phi}{\pi}\,\frac{\beta}{\alpha^2+\beta^2} & -\frac{\phi}{\pi}\,\frac{\alpha}{\alpha^2+\beta^2} \\ \frac{\alpha}{\sqrt{\alpha^2+\beta^2}} & \frac{\beta}{\sqrt{\alpha^2+\beta^2}} \end{bmatrix}$$

For a general treatment, see Bishop, Fienberg and Holland[32], and Rao[33],
Then V can be expressed as

$$V = \begin{bmatrix} A_1 & 0 \\ 0 & I \end{bmatrix} \begin{bmatrix} \Sigma_1 & \Sigma_2 \\ \Sigma_2' & \Sigma_3 \end{bmatrix} \begin{bmatrix} A_1' & 0 \\ 0 & I \end{bmatrix} = \begin{bmatrix} A_1\Sigma_1A_1' & A_1\Sigma_2 \\ \Sigma_2'A_1' & \Sigma_3 \end{bmatrix}$$

Hence standard errors of estimates ordinarily reported using Σ must be reported using V instead, where A_1 is estimated using $\hat{\alpha}$ and $\hat{\beta}$.

In particular,

$$\text{Var}\,\hat{\phi} = a_{11}^2\sigma_{11} + a_{11}a_{12}(\sigma_{21} + \sigma_{12}) + a_{12}^2\sigma_{22}$$

$$= \frac{36}{\pi^2\gamma^4}(\hat{\beta}^2\sigma_{11}{}^2 - 2\rho\hat{\alpha}\hat{\beta}\,\sigma_1\sigma_{22} + \hat{\alpha}^2\sigma_{22}{}^2)$$

$$\text{Var}\,\hat{\gamma} = a_{21}{}^2\sigma_{11}{}^2 + a_{22}a_{21}(\sigma_{21}+\sigma_{12}) + a_{22}{}^2\sigma_{22}{}^2$$

$$= \frac{1}{\gamma^2}(\hat{\alpha}^2\sigma_{11}{}^2 + 2\rho\hat{\alpha}\hat{\beta}\,\sigma_{11}\sigma_{22} + \hat{\beta}^2\sigma_{22}{}^2)$$